Emotional Intelligence

The Complete Psychologist's Guide to Mastering Social Skills, Improve Your Relationships, Boost Your EQ and Self Mastery

Table of Contents

Introduction

I bet if you were asked two decades ago what are the factors that determine a person's overall success in life, you would have said: a high intelligence quotient, good grades, and well-developed cognitive functions. It was natural to assume that people with high intelligence in general had higher chances of being successful. Parents, educators, and peers sang the same tune of high intelligence translating into greater success. We wish it was actually that simple!

If you want to be successful in life, you need to study hard, get awesome grades, go to college, study harder, and graduate with really high honors. This path was believed to be the guaranteed shot to a great job and an abundantly successful life.

You spent years believing this notion, and though it's not completely incorrect, it's not the full picture either. Success is the result of a combination of various factors, and the most fundamental of them is your ability to handle your own and other people's emotions.

1

Emotional intelligence, or emotional quotient, (both represent the same idea), is a type of intelligence that refers to an individual's ability to recognize and manage or control their own and other people's emotions. It is a simple and straightforward concept that comprises two main components:

- Identifying or recognizing emotions, intentions, desires, and goals in yourself and other people.
- Managing these emotions and actions to accomplish the most positive outcome for everyone involved.

Research on emotional intelligence has been ongoing since the mid-20th century within the psycho-scientific community. However, it wasn't until 1995, when Daniel Goleman published his book by the same name, that emotional intelligence rolled into the mainstream consciousness and became a ground-breaking concept. Back then, intelligence quotient was seen as the only factor that mattered when it came to assessing an individual's capabilities. Once emotional intelligence took over, IQ was perceived as a narrow or limited way of assessing an individual's chances of success. The cut-throat world of career, jobs, and business was starkly different from the cushy confines of a classroom.

If one had to navigate the real world, they'd have to adapt to a different kind of intelligence than the academic one used in classrooms or libraries. A person's knowledge and cognitive abilities alone didn't guarantee success in life. A degree didn't automatically mean a high paying job or a profitable business.

At best, you'll get your foot through the door. However, for someone to succeed, you would need much more than just plain intelligence. It would take social, communication, conversation, and emotional skills to raise the bar. These are life skills that don't come in the classroom but are learned by living in a hostel, waiting at bars, joining social clubs, being a part of sports teams, and volunteering.

Do you still think IQ is the only factor that determines a person's overall success in life? If that was true, my friend, every successful person you spot today from the CEO of big organizations to the president, to thought leaders, and successful entrepreneurs should be a Harvard, Stanford, MIT graduate with a Ph.D.

Make a list of ten successful people you admire the most. They are the people you look up to as they lead successful and balanced lives. Are all these folks top honors graduates from distinguished educational institutions with a high IQ? My money is on 'No!'

Again, don't get me wrong here. I am not undermining the importance of intelligence or asking you to shut that book on mechanical engineering and start reading about human psychology. It is awesome if you possess naturally high cognitive abilities and a high intelligence quotient. All I am saying is, you should ideally have both EQ and IQ complementing each other to increase your chances of success in the real world. If you can increase your emotional quotient to back up an already high intelligence quotient, you can achieve many great things!

However, if you ask me to pick between two skills, I would have to go with emotional intelligence. A person with average intelligence and highly evolved emotional intelligence has a greater chance of succeeding in today's world than a person with high intelligence and less developed emotional intelligence. The name of the game today is about managing people, understanding their emotions or motives, and managing their feelings to achieve the most positive results.

Technical knowledge may help you direct or instruct your team when it comes to completing a task. However, your ability to keep them motivated by understanding their emotions will ensure they'll stay inspired and productive throughout the process.

A person's cognitive intelligence or intellectual potential has always been measured as his or her ability to retain facts or make calculations. However, these skills aren't necessarily all-encompassing in certain positions such as leadership and entrepreneurship. Tons of CEOs, world leaders, and Fortune 500 company founders are high-school dropouts. If intelligence alone was the measure of a person's success, how would you explain this?

The reality is that it isn't as straightforward as a single factor like intelligence that determines our success. It is, in fact, a combination of factors which are mainly emotional and social life skills that will help you survive or thrive in the real world.

Intelligence quotient is an inborn, but not all-inclusive, factor that can influence an individual's success in life.

This is good news because, irrespective of your traditional, genetically determined intelligence, you have a good chance of being successful if you work on other social-emotional life skills. A high emotional quotient along with other social and psychological skill sets can definitely boost your chances.

The objective of this book is to discuss crucial aspects of emotional intelligence and how to use them in your everyday life to make your dream of being successful a reality. We'll take a look at practical techniques to raise your emotional quotient and eventually boost your chances of success.

Chapter One: History of Emotional Intelligence Models

Harry and Pete both have a heated argument with their boss. Once Harry gets home, he starts yelling at his children for making noise and not going to bed. On the other hand, Pete doesn't yell or scream at his children even though they are making noise and not in bed yet.

While Harry chides his children rudely for making a mess with their toys, Pete gently, yet assertively, urges them to put their toys in their place and get ready to sleep. Harry doesn't know how to handle his negative emotions that are a direct result of his argument with the boss. He invariably ends up directing that anger towards his children, who aren't connected to the argument in any manner.

Pete understands that he is upset with his boss and not his children. Therefore, there is no point in screaming at his children. It will only make things worse for him.

In the above scenario, both Harry and Pete faced the same emotions, yet the manner in which they expressed a similar emotion differed drastically. Pete was able to identify and manage his emotions differently than Harry, who allowed his emotions to get the better of him.

This is the essence of emotional intelligence. Being able to recognize your own and other people's emotions and the ability to manage these emotions effectively to create a positive and pleasant outcome.

Essentially, emotional intelligence (EQ) is the knack of perceiving, managing, and evaluating emotions to create the desired positive outcome. The term was made popular by Daniel Goleman in 1995 with his ground-breaking book of the same name. However, emotional intelligence as a term was first used by Michael Beldoch in the mid-20th century.

It is the ability to monitor not just your own, but also other people's feelings, distinguish between emotions, label feelings, and leverage this emotional information to direct your thoughts and actions. This is a broader and more general definition of emotional intelligence, though there are differences within the scientific community about what it encompasses. The unanimous view is that it is a skill that involves identifying, understanding, and managing emotions.

Emotional intelligence ability model

The emotional intelligence model was created by Mayer and Salovey, who defined emotional quotient as the ability to correctly recognize, evaluate, and generate emotions to facilitate thought, gain a better understanding of emotions, and manage emotions for enhancing both cognitive and emotional development.

The psychologist duo believed that an individual must be assessed on four distinct interconnected abilities to determine their overall EQ. The four abilities are:

- **Recognizing emotions**
  This involves picking up verbal and non-verbal clues for understanding a person's emotions.

- **Reasoning or using these emotions to facilitate thinking and intellectual activity**

  For example, leveraging emotions to offer solutions or reviewing situations. This helps us focus our limited attention span on the right things and react as per the situation. This benefits the overall creative process.

- **Understanding emotions**

  Human emotions are complex. They hold multiple meanings and guide us in understanding another person's emotional state of mind. They help us understand other people's emotions and why people feel the way they do. Emotions have several nuances and aren't often as straightforward as they appear. Every emotion holds its own pattern of thoughts, actions, and intentions.

  For example, if a person is hurt, you will be able to deduce why he or she feels hurt. An individual with this particular ability can immediately understand another person's emotional state and why they are thinking or behaving in a certain manner.

- **Regulating emotions**

  This is the ability to manage your own and other people's emotions by responding suitably to them. For instance, you know how to react appropriately when a person is angry or upset. In the example at the beginning of the chapter, we saw how Pete was able to regulate his emotions positively, even though both he and Harry experienced similar emotions. Controlling our own and other people's emotions is a major component of emotional intelligence.

Salovey-Mayer concluded that an individual may be closed to emotional signals that are too painful or uncomfortable while being open to those that aren't overwhelming. This is calculated through the Mayer-Salovey-Caruso Emotional Intelligence Test (MESCEIT). It is measured by emotion-focused problem-solving.

Mixed model emotional intelligence

This model of emotional intelligence was founded on Daniel Goleman's 25 distinct emotional intelligence traits, which encompasses everything from teamwork, service orientation, and accomplishment motivation to self-awareness.

It is referred to as a mixed model since it merges emotional intelligence traits with other personality characteristics that are linked neither with emotion nor intelligence. Emotional competence is a capability that can be learned and developed to create outstanding results. This emotional intelligence model is based on five primary categories, each one with clear emotional competencies:

- **Self-awareness**

  Self-awareness is the ability to identify an emotion as we experience it. We tune in to our inner selves for assessing what exactly we are feeling and how to best regulate it. Self-awareness comprises self-confidence in your capabilities and emotional awareness in realizing what you are feeling and the subsequent emotional effects.

- **Self-regulation**

  We think we don't have great control over our emotions, but negative emotions can be managed through various self-regulating techniques like walking, prayer, running, and meditation. To self-regulate effectively, one needs to have control over their impulsive actions, must demonstrate honesty and integrity, possess creative thinking, must be able to handle change easily, and can take responsibility for their actions.

- **Motivation**

  Motivation is the ability to work towards fulfilling a set of goals. The most important aspect of this category is positive thinking. To become a positive thinker, one must always stay positive and be capable of restructuring negative thoughts. This can be accomplished by optimism, commitment, initiative, and drive for achievement. You are perpetually involved in the pursuit of improving yourself to become a better person.

- **Empathy**

  Empathy is a huge component of emotional intelligence. It is the ability to not just discern people's emotions but also to 'feel' what they feel. Empathy is about understanding others, being able to anticipate other people's needs, helping others develop their qualities, and building relationships with people who are quite different from you. Empathy is comprised of more than a single ability. However, fundamentally, it is about being able to feel and relate to other people's emotions.

- **Social skills**

  Relating to other people is another important attribute of emotional intelligence. Social skills are important in teamwork, collaboration, communication, influence, building relationships, and conflict management.

This emotional quotient model measures emotional intelligence with the 'Emotional Competence Inventory' and 'Emotional Intelligence Appraisal.'

Emotional intelligence trait model

The trait type emotional intelligence model was developed by Petrides (and his co-workers) in 2009 to assess emotional quotient. It shifts from the previous ability-based model and talks about how people possess specific emotional characteristics or traits and self-perceptions based on their unique personality.

Basically, emotional intelligence is an individual's self-perceptions about their emotional capabilities, behavior, actions, and abilities. Another label for the same concept is emotional self-efficiency. These traits aren't assessed in the real scientific way. Rather, they are analyzed by a respondent's self-analysis. The 'Trait Emotional Questionnaire' measures an individual's ability to accurately list their own traits.

Brief history of emotional intelligence

The term 'emotional intelligence' was first coined by Peter Salovey and John D. Mayer in 1990, describing it as a type of social intelligence involving the ability to regulate one's own emotions as well as other people's feelings and emotions, to differentiate among these emotions, and to utilize this information for guiding one's thoughts and actions.

Salovey and Mayer launched a research program for measuring a person's emotional intelligence and exploring its significance. For example, there was a study conducted on a group of people, where it was discovered that people who can identify and give a clear name to emotions were able to recover easily from an upsetting film they'd watched.

In another experiment, people who scored high in their ability to perceive things correctly and identify or understand other people's emotions were able to respond more effectively to changes within their social circle and build social support networks.

During the early 90s, Daniel Goleman became acquainted with Salovey and Mayer's research, which led him to author *Emotional Intelligence*. Goleman's school of emotional intelligence believed that it wasn't cognitive intelligence that guaranteed a person's business success, but a person's ability to manage his own and other people's emotions that determined his chances of success. He stated that emotionally intelligent people possess four primary characteristics:

1. People with high emotional intelligence are good at identifying their emotions or have good self-awareness.
2. They mastered the ability to manage their emotions.
3. They were able to show empathy to the emotions of other people.
4. They were efficient at handling other's emotions.

The seeds of emotional intelligence were sown way back in the 1930s when the concept of 'social intelligence' was put forth by Edward Thorndike. He described it as the ability to form interpersonal and social relationships with people.

In the 1940s, David Wechsler suggested that attributes of effective intelligence may be responsible for success.

During the 1950s, humanistic psychologist Abraham Maslow described how people can develop emotional strength.

In 1953, people started thinking about emotions and intelligence. Dorothy Van Ghent described how novels such as

Jane Austen's *Pride and Prejudice* featured characters with high emotional intelligence.

In 1975, Howard Gardner published *The Shattered Mind*, which discussed the concept of different types of intelligence apart from cognitive intelligence.

In 1987, *Mensa Magazine* published an article in which Keith Beasley uses "emotional quotient" as a phrase for the first time. This was the first published use of the term, though Reuven Bar-on claimed to use the term in his unpublished thesis prior to the Mensa article.

In 1990, Peter Salovey and John Meyer's ground-breaking article on emotional intelligence is published.

In 1995, the concept of Emotional Intelligence is made popular all over the world after *New York Times* writer Daniel Goleman's publication of *Emotional Intelligence: Why It Can Matter More Than IQ*. Goleman drew from Salovey and Meyer's research to talk about emotional intelligence as a vital type of intelligence for success in academics and work.

One of the most crucial aspects of emotional intelligence is that, unlike intelligence quotient, emotional intelligence is not fixed. While some people are born with an aptitude for various emotional and social components, emotional intelligence is largely malleable.

Emotional intelligence experts agree that conventional intelligence contributes to a mere 10-25 percent of our success. A major chunk of it, however, is determined by multiple factors, including our ability to manage our own and other people's emotions.

Research conducted by Harvard graduates across several professions, including medicine and law, concluded there was a zero and, at times, a negative correlation between high entrance test scores and success in various professions. This clearly establishes that a high intelligence quotient, or knowledge, alone doesn't determine a person's chances of succeeding.

Research headed by Dr. Travis Bradberry concluded that 90 percent of top performing workers in an organization possess high emotional intelligence. People with high emotional quotient also earn $29,000 more annually than their counterparts with low emotional intelligence within the same profession. Thus, people with high emotional intelligence are not only more productive and efficient but also, on an average, make more money than people with low emotional intelligence.

Goleman's emotional intelligence framework

Goleman's emotional intelligence framework focuses on the idea that emotional quotient, or intelligence, is an important factor in personal, professional, and social success. The framework states that emotional quotient has five fundamental domains which are then divided into four separate quadrants. A couple of these domains are linked to personal abilities, while the remaining two are linked with social competencies.

Goleman's theory is popular worldwide because it speaks of emotional intelligence as an ability that can be developed in contrast to intelligence quotient, which is largely predetermined by genetic factors.

While personal competencies are categorized into self-awareness and self-management, social competencies are divided into social awareness and relationship management.

Self-awareness is the ability to identify your own emotions and their impact on yourself and others around you. Self-regulation, or management, is about managing or regulating your emotions to ensure emotions don't end up controlling you.

Social awareness includes organizational awareness, service orientation, and empathy. Relationship management includes leadership, inspiring and developing others, influence, change catalyst, building connections, teamwork, communication, and collaboration.

Self-awareness

Self-awareness is the ability to recognize one's feelings and their consequences. People with high self-awareness possess the following competencies:

- They know the emotions they are experiencing and why they are experiencing these emotions.

- They recognize how their emotions impact their performance.

- They are aware of their strengths and limitations.

- Self-aware people are open to constructive criticism or feedback, fresher perspectives, constant learning, and personal development.

- They are decisive by nature and can make clear decisions even when they're under stress and faced with uncertainties.

- People with high self-awareness are able to establish the connection between people's feelings, thoughts, and actions.

- They are able to display a sense a of humor and view themselves from a lighter perspective. People who indulge in self-deprecating humor are often confident, self-assured, and emotionally intelligent people.

- People with high self-awareness do not feel the need to go with the tide. They are happy to stand alone and voice views that do not match popular views.

Self-regulation

Self-regulation is the ability to manage disturbing emotions and emotional impulses that can hinder interpersonal relationships and performance. Here are some competencies that people with high self-regulation possess:

- People with high emotional self-control can manage their impulses and disturbing emotions effectively.

- They are able to stay calm, positive, and unaffected even in the most trying circumstances.

- People with high self-regulation are able to build trust and credibility through reliability, integrity, and authenticity. They are also able to accept their own mistakes and are brave enough to call out others for their unethical acts.

- High self-regulation abilities lead these people to meet commitments, keep promises, and act on their word.

- They are also highly effective in handling change and adapting to new scenarios.

Social awareness

Social awareness is understanding other people's feelings and views and taking a keen interest in their concerns as if it is one's own concern. People who have high empathy possess the following abilities:

- They are extremely perceptive to verbal and nonverbal emotional clues while listening to people.

- They show understanding for another person's point of view even though they may not necessarily agree with it.

- They are happy to help solve people's problems and concerns in any manner within their capacity.

- People with high social awareness acknowledge other people's accomplishments and reward them for their strengths.

Social skills

Social skills are the ability to influence and persuade people. People with high social skills possess the following competencies:

- They are able to deal with conflicts in an assertive and straightforward manner.

- They practice open communication and are receptive to both praise and criticism.

- People with high social skills can inspire others to pursue a shared goal or vision.

Impact of emotional intelligence in daily life — examples

Let us say you've been offered constructive feedback by your manager about areas you can improve upon or areas where you didn't perform to your fullest potential. People with a low emotional quotient may take the criticism personally or come up with a host of excuses and blame games to cover their shortcomings. They may not accept their mistakes or they may find a scapegoat to blame their inefficacy on. They may get angry, irritable, depressed, and demotivated. Acting on emotions is easier. Identifying them and regulating them takes work.

Conversely, an individual with greater emotional intelligence will accept the fact that no one is perfect. Rather than taking the feedback personally, they'll introspect about what their manager said and work on areas of improvement to become more efficient. They will stop making similar mistakes. People with a high emotional quotient will actively seek feedback from others rather than focus on proving themselves right. They are less likely to argue and blame others for their shortcomings.

Emotionally intelligent people are open to suggestions and constructive feedback, which eventually helps them accomplish their objectives. For these folks, being right is being more efficient. They value feedback and actively work on it. This is just one of the ways high emotional intelligence can positively affect your productivity and success in the workplace.

Let us now take another example in a personal scenario.

You are involved in a heated discussion about political ideologies with your best friend. While your friend is fervently putting forth their views about their ideology, you firmly stick to your opinion. When they speak, they appear angry. An emotionally intelligent person can quickly gauge this emotion and understand the impact of the topic on their friend. You realize that you could end up hurting or upsetting them if the topic continues for a while.

A person with high emotional intelligence gets a grip on the circumstances easily and gently acknowledges the other person's view even if they don't necessarily subscribe to those ideas. They may not agree with their friend, but they are accepting their right to disagree. Since this person is more thoughtful, empathetic, and sensitive to other people's needs, they can successfully stop a discussion from blowing into a full-fledged fight. Thus, things finish on a constructive and positive note.

Now, consider the same scenario with a person who isn't emotionally intelligent or empathetic towards other people's feelings. This kind of person is adamantly focused on their views. They refuse to understand where the other person is coming from. Thus, the discussion snowballs into a heated argument. They fan the flame of the difference even more. The results are anger, hurt, and negativity. The fight ends badly and affects their interpersonal relationship.

We can all identify that one emotionally intelligent person within our family, friends, or social circle. They always say the most appropriate thing to say in any situation. They can pacify people, thwart potentially uncomfortable situations, nip arguments in the bud, and arrive at a solution where everyone is pleased. Irrespective of how tricky a scenario is, they manage to find their way through it by using emotional information about their own and other people's feelings.

They excel in handling challenging situations that involve differences between people and know how to assert themselves without offending anyone. These are the empathetic, considerate, and caring folks who also know how to assert themselves. Any wonder that most companies today demand people with high emotional intelligence for filling leadership positions?

While people with a high intelligence quotient may have the answer or solution to your problems, emotionally intelligent people can make you feel more hopeful about the situation.

Chapter Two: Solid Tips for Boosting Emotional Self-awareness

The first step towards developing greater emotional intelligence is boosting self-awareness, or your understanding of your own feelings and emotions. You can regulate your emotions for an optimally positive outcome only if you are able to identify these emotions. Labeling emotions and determining your actions based on these emotions is critical to the process of developing emotional intelligence. When you are more aware of your feelings and emotions, recognizing other people's emotions becomes simpler.

Here are solid, proven tips for boosting self-awareness to get you started on the path of emotional intelligence:

Label your emotions

Label and categorize your emotions. I know this makes your feelings sound like they belong to a library. However, labeling, or giving names to your emotions, makes it easier to identify and act upon them. When you feel an emotion surging through you, attempt to identify it quickly. Is it fear, insecurity, jealousy, anger, elation, depression, surprise, or a combination of these emotions?

Identify the triggers that cause these emotions. For instance, a specific person may evoke jealousy in you because you feel they are more successful than you.

What makes you feel certain emotions? What are the triggers that anger or hurt you? What makes you happy and sad? What is the source of positive and destructive emotions in you? Labeling your feelings and recognizing the stimuli for various emotions will increase your emotional self-awareness.

Grab a pen and paper to list your emotions when you experience a compelling feeling. Mention the precise emotion or feeling that you are experiencing. Accompany this emotional label with the trigger that caused it. What is it that made you feel the way you do? When you recognize an emotion, it is easier to manage it.

For instance, let us assume you feel a deep sense of loathing for a person without any specific reason. You dislike them and can't stand them, but funnily, can't tell why you dislike them. Upon closer examination of your feelings, you realize you dislike them because you are envious of them. You may believe they are always having a wonderful life, while things never go your way. By nailing this emotion as jealousy, you can regulate your potentially negative emotions.

Once you recognize the emotion as irrational jealousy, you will view it in a more logical and understanding manner. You'll begin to think along the lines that it isn't really someone's fault that they lead an amazing life. In fact, they should be applauded for working hard towards their goals. You'll realize that no one has a perfect life. Everyone goes through shares of trials and tribulation to attain success, which isn't necessarily visible to the outside world. Sometimes, it is only how we perceive things and not the reality. Thus, once you are more mindful of your emotions, you can work with them more positively.

Be an expert on yourself

What is the one thing you should do to bring about changes in your thoughts, actions, and behavior? The answer is: awareness about these thoughts and subsequent actions! To make changes, you ought to know what you have to improve upon.

Knowing yourself inside out is the key to being more emotionally aware and savvy. Did you know athletes are trained to identify and overcome feelings before an important upcoming game? This is based on the premise that if you can successfully identify and control your emotions, it doesn't impact your productivity.

Go back and think about all the recent instances where you let emotions get the better of you and affect your productivity. Haven't you let trivial matters impact your performance?

By being aware of your strengths and weaknesses, it is easier to confidently accomplish your objectives. There is a lesser scope for frustration, low productivity, and disappointment. Self-confidence increases your assertiveness while you express your thoughts and opinions, which is important for developing social skills.

Once you gain greater awareness, you will rarely be ruled by emotions. You have a clear edge if you are able to regulate your emotions. An emotionally aware person stops being a victim of his emotions and uses these emotions in a positive way to reach a desired outcome.

Spend time recognizing areas of development to strengthen them

- List all your strengths and weaknesses.
- Take a formal, psychological personality assessment test that helps you discover your own skills, abilities, limitations, and values.
- Obtain objective feedback from people you trust.

One way that works wonders for increasing your self-awareness is journaling. Write in a flowing stream of consciousness about the thoughts you are feeling and experiencing as they are occurring. What are the emotions you are experiencing? What are the physiological reactions to your feelings? Are you experiencing a faster heartbeat, sweaty palms, increased pulse, etc. as a physical reaction to your emotions?

Emotions aren't always straightforward. In fact, they are complex and multi-layered. For example, you may have a heated argument with your partner and feel angry, hurt, upset, and vengeful all at the same time. Write emotions exactly as you are experiencing them, even if two emotions appear to contradict each other. For instance, if you've got a scholarship to study overseas, you may be elated at the opportunity. However, the thought of leaving behind your partner may cause a twinge of sadness, too. You are acknowledging and validating your emotions by writing them.

Dexter Valles, the CEO of Valmar International, suggests carrying a whiteboard divided into two to three parts throughout the day. Add six to eight feelings to the board and ask employees to put a check on the feelings they experience at different points during the day. Determine which emotions have the maximum check marks.

Make a list of every role you play in your daily life such as being a parent, sibling, volunteer, worker, and more. What are the emotions linked with each role? For example, you may enjoy your role as a parent, but you can also be an unhappy employee. Examine every role and the emotions attached to it carefully.

Naming emotions linked to every relationship will help you manage emotions within that relationship more efficiently. It will keep you in greater control of your emotional reaction where the specific role is concerned.

Do a frequent check-in

Do a frequent check-in with your emotions much like how you have a waiter checking in with you frequently to know if you need anything. You do a mental check-in of your emotions periodically to understand how you are feeling at different times during the day. It is a sort of, "Hello, mind, how are you feeling? What can be done to make you feel better?"

Examine the origin of these specific feelings. Are you feeling low and deflated because your boss said something to you in the morning? Are you feeling angry and hurt because you fought with your partner? Are you experiencing certain physiological symptoms as a result of these emotions or feelings? Are these emotions impacting your body language, posture, gestures, and expressions? Are these emotions evident or visible to others? Are you more transparent when it comes to expressing your emotions? Are your decisions primarily determined by emotions?

If you want to be a more emotionally balanced person, reconnect with your primary emotions, recognize them, accept the emotions, and use them for making better decisions.

Use third person

Research in the field of labeling our emotions has indicated that when we distance ourselves from our emotions, or view them more objectively, we gain higher self-awareness. Next time you feel the urge to say, "I am disappointed," try to say, "Jack is disappointed."

If that seems too preposterous, try saying, "I am presently experiencing sadness," or, "One of my feelings at the moment is sadness."

These are techniques through which you are distancing yourself from overpowering emotions to stay naturally composed. You are basically treating your emotions as just another piece of information rather than being overwhelmed by them.

Each time you find yourself experiencing an urge to react to a situation, take a moment to name it. Then use it in the third person to distance yourself from intense emotions.

Emotions don't always need to be fixed

You don't always have to identify emotions with the intention of fixing them. Self-awareness is not about fixing emotions. It is about recognizing these emotions and letting them pass rather than allowing them to get the better of you. Society has conditioned us to think that certain emotions are bad. We mistakenly believe that experiencing these emotions makes us a bad person.

Far from it, emotions aren't good or bad. They are just that, emotions. There's no need to push away the seemingly bad emotions. Acknowledge that you are experiencing an emotion by saying something like, "I am experiencing jealousy." Practice deep breathing for a while until the emotion passes. Rather than pushing the emotion away and, in the process, increasing its intensity to come back even stronger, gently acknowledge it and let it be until it passes.

It takes around six seconds for the body to absorb chemicals that can alter your emotions. Give your body that much time.

We often share a hostile relationship with our emotions. They are believed to be something that is negative and should be fought or suppressed. However, emotions are information that helps us function in our daily lives. Overcome the mindset that emotions are good or bad, and instead focus on using them to empower you. Rather than letting emotions take control of you, use emotional information to work with them.

Emotions are neural hormones that are released as a direct response to our perceptions regarding the world. They direct us towards a specific action. All emotions have a distinct message and objective, which means there's no such thing as a good or bad emotion.

For example, fear helps us focus on an impending danger and take the necessary action to defend ourselves. Similarly, sadness makes us experience a sense of loss and facilitates a better understanding of what we truly care about.

If you move away from your best friend and become sad, this mean you truly care about them so much that you experienced sadness. This is valuable information. Hence, sadness is not a bad emotion. It can be used to identify what you care about.

If you use emotions as information for recognizing feelings, they can be channeled positively. The number one rule for developing higher emotional intelligence is to stop judging and curbing your emotions.

Train yourself to identify emotions based on physiological reactions

Our emotions often have physical manifestations. For example, you may feel anxious before a job interview or an important presentation. You experience the sensation of having 'butterflies in your stomach' before addressing an audience on the stage.

Don't you find your heart pounding with excitement when you are about to go on a date with someone you've fancied for long? Nervousness leaves us with sweaty palms and stiff muscles.

While these are only some of the physiological reactions we experience with our emotions, research has proven that a variety of emotions are strongly associated with stimulating certain parts of the body.

Regular patterns of physical sensations are linked with each of the six fundamental emotions, including fear, happiness, anger, sadness, disgust, and surprise. Human emotions discreetly overlap physiological sensations. For example, lower limb sensations are associated with sadness. Similarly, increased upper limb sensations are connected with anger. A strong feeling of disgust generates sensations within the throat and digestive system. Fear and surprise generate sensations in the chest.

Identify recurring patterns

This can be one of the most effective parts of knowing yourself. Neuroscience will help you understand the process more effectively. Our brains have an inherent tendency to follow established neural paths rather than creating new ones. This doesn't necessarily mean that the established patterns are serving us positively or that they can't be altered.

For instance, when a person becomes angry, he or she may bottle up their emotion rather than express it. This has become an emotional pattern with the person and is deeply embedded in the mind. However, awareness of this pattern can help the person chart another course of action, where the person practices responding instead of simply reacting to the emotion. However, the first step to charting a new pattern is identifying a pattern.

Recognize the build-up of emotions before something suddenly triggers you. These triggers have a predictable pattern. If you are already frustrated, you are more likely to see a situation in a more negative light. Similarly, if you are overcome by fear, you are more likely to interpret a stimulus as a threat. It is therefore important to be aware of these biases and how they can impact our emotions by creating a predictable pattern. The more efficient you become in recognizing your biases, the lower your chances of misinterpreting a stimulus.

Work with what you know about emotions

Emotions are important pieces of data that help you gauge things from a clearer and objective perspective. Don't suppress, ignore, fight, or feel overwhelmed by your emotions. Instead, you should build a valuable library of experiences with them. The purpose of emotional awareness is to concentrate our attention on these emotions and use them positively to create the desired outcome.

Treat your emotions as data that relies on your view of the world, or as a guide on how to act. When you open yourself to this data, you enjoy access to a huge resource of emotions that can be utilized to drive your actions in the right direction. You will know exactly how to reach wherever it is that you want to go if you have a clear emotional route. Therefore, you should acknowledge and recognize your emotions as data, and work with them instead of trying to beat them.

Begin by carefully noticing how you feel at the moment. Observe emotions without judging them or attempting to fix them. Learn to simply notice your emotions.

Be receptive to feedback and constructive criticism

One of the best ways to develop greater awareness of your emotions is to be more open to feedback and criticism from others. For instance, a friend may tell you that each time they talk about their accomplishments they sense your pangs of envy or dislike towards them. This may help you tune into your emotions and emotional triggers more effectively.

Emotionally intelligent folks are open to receiving feedback, and they always consider the other person's point of view. You may not necessarily agree with them, but listening to other people's criticism and feedback helps you work on your blind spots. This can help you recognize your thoughts, triggers, and behavioral patterns.

I know a person who, in a bid to increase his self-awareness and emotional quotient, actively goes around asking people for feedback about his words, feelings (as they understand it), and actions. It acts as an emotion meter, which helps him gain greater awareness of his emotions and regulate them more efficiently.

Chapter Three: Emotional Intelligence and Delaying Gratification

I am guessing you do know about the famous 'marshmallow test' of emotional intelligence. If you don't, here it is:

During the 1960s, social psychologist Walter Mischel headed several psychological studies on delayed rewards and gratification. He closely studied hundreds of children between the ages of 4 to 5 years to reveal a trait that is known to be one of the most important factors that determine success in a person's life, gratification.

This experiment is famously referred to as the marshmallow test. The experiment involved introducing every child into a private chamber and placing a single marshmallow in front of them. At this stage, the researcher struck a deal with the child.

The researcher informed them that he would be gone from the chamber for a while. The child was then informed that if he or she didn't eat the marshmallow while the researcher was away, he would come back and reward them with an additional marshmallow apart from the one on the table. However, if they did eat the marshmallow placed on the table in front of them, they wouldn't be rewarded with another.

It was clear. One marshmallow immediately or two marshmallows later.

The researcher walked out of the chamber and re-entered after 15 minutes.

Predictably, some children leaped on the marshmallow in front of them and ate it as soon as the researcher walked out of the room. However, others tried hard to restrain themselves by diverting their attention. They bounced, jumped around, and scooted on the chairs to distract themselves in a bid to stop themselves from eating the marshmallow. However, many of these children failed to resist the temptation and eventually gave in.

Only a handful of children managed to hold until the very end without eating the marshmallow.

The study was published in 1972 and became globally popular as 'The Marshmallow Experiment.' However, it doesn't end here. The real twist in the tale is what followed several years later.

Researchers undertook a follow-up study to track the life and progress of each child who was a part of the initial experiment. They studied several areas of the person's life and were surprised by what they discovered. The children who delayed gratification for higher rewards or waited until the end to earn two marshmallows instead of one had higher school grades, lower instances of substance abuse, lower chances of obesity, and better stress coping abilities.

The research was known as a ground-breaking study on gratification because researchers followed up on the children 40 years after the initial experiment was conducted, and it was sufficiently evident that the group of children who delayed gratification patiently for higher rewards succeeded in all areas they were measured on.

This experiment proved beyond doubt that delaying gratification is one of the most crucial skills for success in life.

Success and delaying gratification

Success usually boils down to picking between the discomfort of discipline over the pleasure or comfort of distraction. This is exactly what delaying gratification is. Would you rather go out for the new movie in town where all your friends are heading, or would you rather sit up and study for an examination to earn good grades? Would you rather party hard with your co-workers before the team gets started with an important upcoming presentation? Or would you sit late and work on fine tuning the presentation?

Our ability to delay gratification is also a huge factor when it comes to decision making and is considered an important aspect of emotional intelligence. Each day, we make several choices and decisions. While some are trivial and have little influence on our future (what color shoes should I buy? Or which way should I take to work?), others have a huge bearing on our success and future.

As human beings, we are wired to make decisions or choices that offer an instant return on investment. We want quick results, actions, and rewards. The mind is naturally tuned for a short-term profit. Why do you think e-commerce giants are making a killing by charging an additional fee for same day and next day delivery? Today is better than tomorrow!

Think about how different our life would be if we thought about the impact of our decisions about three to five years from now? If we can bring about this mental shift where we can delay gratification by keeping our eyes firmly fixated on the bigger picture several years from now, our lives can be very different.

Another factor that is important in gratification delay is the environment. For example, if children who were able to resist temptation were not given a second marshmallow or reward for delaying gratification, they are less likely to view delaying gratification as a positive habit.

If parents do not keep their commitment to reward a child for delaying gratification, the child won't value the trait. Delaying gratification can be picked up only in an environment of commitment and trust, where a second marshmallow is given when deserved.

Examples of gratification delay

Let us say you want to buy your dream car that you see in the showroom on your way to work every day. You imagine how wonderful it would be to own and drive that car. The car costs $25,000, and you barely have $5000 dollars in your current savings. How do you buy the car then? Simple, you start saving. This is how you will combine strong willpower with delayed gratification.

There are countless opportunities for you to blow money every day such as hitting the bar with friends for a drink on weekends, co-workers visiting the nearest coffee shop to grab a latte, or buying expensive gadgets. Every time you remove your wallet to pay, you have two clear choices: either blow your money on monetary pleasure or wait for the long-term reward. If you can resist these temptations and curtail your expenses, you'll be closer to purchasing your dream car. Making this decision will help you buy a highly desirable thing in future.

Will you spend now for immediate gratifications and pleasures, or will you save to buy something more valuable in the future?

Here is another interesting example to elucidate the concept of delayed gratification. Let us say you want to be the best film director the world has ever seen. You want to master the craft and pick up all skills related to movie making and the entertainment business. You visualize yourself as making spectacular movies that inspire and entertain people for decades.

How do you plan to work towards a large goal, or the big picture (well, literally)? You'll start by doing mundane, boring, uninspiring jobs on the sets such as being someone's assistant, fetching them a cup of coffee, cleaning the sets, and other similar boring chores. It isn't exciting or fun, but you go through it each day because you have your eyes firmly fixated on the larger goal, or bigger picture.

You know you want to become a huge filmmaker one day and are prepared to delay gratification for fulfilling that goal. The discomfort of your current life is smaller in comparison to the pleasure of the higher goal. This is delayed gratification. Despite the discomfort, you regulate your actions and behavior for meeting a bigger goal in the future. It may be tough and boring currently, but you know that doing these arduous tasks will give you that shot to make it big someday.

Delayed gratification can be applicable in all aspects of life from health to relationships. Almost every decision we make involves a decision between opting for short-term pleasures now and enjoying bigger rewards later. A burger can give you immediate pleasure today, whereas an apple may not give you instant pleasure but will benefit your body in the long run.

Stop drop technique

Each time you identify an overpowering or stressful emotion that is compelling you to seek immediate pleasure, describe your feelings by writing them down. Make sure you state them clearly to acknowledge their existence.

Have you seen the old VCR models? They had a big pause button prominently placed in the middle. You are now going to push the pause button on your thoughts.

Focus all attention on the heart as it is the center of all your feelings.

Think of something remarkably beautiful that you experienced. It can be a spectacular sunset you witnessed on one of your trips, a beautiful flower you saw in a garden today, or a cute pet kitten you spotted in the neighborhood. Basically, anything that evokes feelings of joy, happiness, and positivity in you. The idea is to bring about a shift in your feelings.

Experience the feeling for some time and allow it to linger. Imagine the feelings you experience in and around your heart. If it is still challenging, take deep breaths. Hold the positive feeling and enjoy it.

Now, click on the mental pause button and revisit the compelling idea that was causing stressful feelings. How does it feel right now?

Now write down how you are feeling and what comes to mind. Act on the fresh insight if it is suitable.

This process doesn't take much time (again, you are craving instant gratification) and makes it easier for you to resist giving in to temptation. The real trick is to change the physical feeling with the heart to bring about a shift in thoughts and eventually, actions. You don't suffocate or undermine your emotions.

Rather, you acknowledge them and then gently change them. When your emotions are slowly changing, the brain tows its line which makes us think in a way that lets us act according to our values and not on impulse or uncontrollable emotions.

Self-mastery is the master key

According to Walter Mischel, "Goal-directed and self-imposed gratification delay is fundamental to the process of emotional self-regulation." Emotional management, or regulation and the ability to control one's impulses, are vital to the concept of emotional intelligence.

Mischel's research established that while some people are born with a greater control for impulses, or better emotional management, others are not. A majority of people are somewhere in between. However, the good news is that emotional management, unlike intelligence, can be learned through practice. EQ isn't as genetically determined as cognitive abilities.

Impulse control and delayed gratification

Have you ever said something in anger and then regretted it immediately? Have you ever acted on an impulse or in haste only to regret it soon after the act? I can't even count the number of people who have lost their jobs, ruined their relationships, nixed their business negotiations, and blown away friendships because of that one moment when they acted on impulse. When you don't allow thoughts to take over and control your words or actions, you demonstrate low emotional intelligence.

Thus, the concept of emotional intelligence is closely connected with delaying gratification. We've all acted at some point or another without worrying about the consequences of our actions. Impulse control, or the ability to construct our thoughts and actions prior to speaking or acting, is a huge part of emotional control. You can manage your emotions more efficiently when you learn to override impulses, which is why impulse control is a huge part of emotional intelligence.

Ever wondered about the reason behind counting to ten, 100, or 1000 before reacting each time you are angry? We've all had our parents and educators counsel us about how anger can be restrained by counting up to ten or 100. It is simple, while you are in the process of counting, your emotional level is slowly decreasing. Once you are done with counting, the overpowering impulse to react to the emotion has passed. This allows you act in a more rational and thoughtful manner.

Emotional intelligence is about identifying these impulsive reactions and regulating them in a more positive and constructive manner. Rather than reacting mindlessly to a situation, you need to stop and think before responding. You choose to respond carefully instead of reacting impulsively to accomplish a more positive outcome or thwart a potentially uncomfortable situation.

Here are some useful tips for delaying gratification and boosting your ability to regulate emotions:

- **Have a clear vision for your future**
  Delaying gratification and controlling impulses or emotions becomes easier when you have a clear picture of

the future. When you know what you want to accomplish five, eight, ten, or 15 years from now, it will be a lot easier to keep the bigger picture in mind if you come across temptations that can ruin your goal. Your 'why' (compelling reason for accomplishing a goal) will keep you sustained throughout the process of meeting the goal. Have a plan to fulfill your goal once you have a clear goal in mind. Identifying your goals and planning how you'll get there will help you resist the temptation more effectively.

- **Find ways to distract yourself from temptations and eliminate triggers**

  For instance, if you are planning to quit drinking, take a different route back home from work if there are several bars along the way. Instead of focusing on what you can't do, concentrate on the activities you are passionate about. Surround yourself with positive people and activities that will help you dwell on your goal. Avoid trying to fill your time with material goods.

- **Make spending money difficult**

  If you are a slave to plastic money and online transactions, you are making the process of spending money too easy for your own good. Paying with cold, hard cash can make you think several times before spending. You'll reconsider your purchases when you pay with real money rather than plastic. Take a part of your salary and put it into a separate account that you won't touch. Make sure that accessing your savings account won't be easy.

- **Avoid 'all or nothing' thinking**

  Most of us think resisting temptation or giving up a bad habit is an 'all or nothing challenge.' It is natural for a majority of normal human beings to have a minor slip here and there. However, that doesn't mean you should just fall off and quit. Occasional slip-ups shouldn't be used as an excuse to get off the track. Despite a small detour, you can get back on the track. Don't try to convince yourself to wander in the opposite direction.

- **Make a list of common rationalizations**

  Find a counterpoint or counterargument for each. For example, you were angry for just five minutes, or you are spending only ten dollars extra. Tell yourself that five minutes of anger is 150 minutes a month wasted in anger or ten dollars extra is $3,000 extra spent throughout the year.

Chapter Four: Boost Your Social EQ with These Powerful Verbal and Non-Verbal Clues

We've established in earlier chapters how emotional intelligence is the master key to effective leadership and social skills. By tuning into other people's emotions or by empathizing with how they feel, there is a higher chance that you will respond appropriately to create the desired positive result. Thus, our ability to connect with our own and other people's emotions can be a powerful tool in social and leadership situations.

Understanding other people, helping overcome stress situations, motivating your team, negotiating business deals, and building a close-knit social circle becomes easier when you can use the emotional information you have about them as leverage. It increases situational awareness and our ability to read people, thus helping us make the most positive decision.

Here are some verbal and non-verbal factors impacting social-emotional quotient, or our ability to read and deal with people:

Body language

Research reveals that body language accounts for 50 percent of our communication. You'd wonder why there were words in the first place if body language accounts for half the communication process. Tuning in to a person's body language will help you pick up important signals related to their emotional state and subconscious thoughts or feelings.

Here's a quick cue sheet to reading people's feelings through their body language:

- Crossed arms and legs are signals of people creating a subconscious barrier. They are emotionally closed, suspicious, or do not subscribe to your ideas. They aren't open to listening to your views or are disinterested in the topic of conversation. You may have to emotionally open the person up a bit by changing the topic and then get back to the original topic. The physical act of uncrossing their arms and legs will make them more subconsciously receptive to your ideas.

- How can you tell a genuine smile from a fake one? Simple, it's all in the eyes. Observe that there's crinkled skin near the person's eyes forming crow's feet. People often present a happy expression to hide their true feelings. However, if their smile doesn't cause the skin around their eyes and mouth to crinkle, they are most likely not as happy as they are pretending to be. Artificial smiles create wrinkles only around the mouth, while genuine smiles create wrinkles around the sides of the eyes.

- When people constantly take their gaze away from you while speaking, they are most likely not being very honest or trying to hide something. Similarly, if a person speaks to you without taking their gaze away from you for long, they may be trying to threaten or intimidate you with their gaze. It is alright to look away periodically. However, shifting gaze constantly is a red flag.

- When you are addressing a group of people, closely observe the ones who are nodding excessively or in a more exaggerated manner. These are the people who are most concerned about your approval. They are anxious about making a positive impression and want to be in your 'good books.'

- People who are nervous or anxious tend to fidget with their hands or objects. Other signs of nervousness also include excessive blinking, tapping feet, and constantly running one's hand over the face.

- When an entire group walks into the room, how do you analyze who the leader or decision maker is? Quickly observe everyone's posture. The leader will most likely walk with a straight posture, with shoulders pulled out. Subconsciously, they are trying to occupy maximum space to convey authority over their team. Standing straight and pulling back shoulders increases a person's physical frame. It makes them come across as much bigger than they actually are. This is why people in power love to keep this posture to show their influence over a group or place.

- Expressions are the windows into a person's emotional state. When a person is amazed or surprised, their eyebrows are raised, and the upper eyelids widen. Similarly, the mouth gapes open. Expressions can often overlap, so watch for micro expressions that can reveal precise emotions.

- For instance, raised eyebrows can also reveal fear. Look for other micro expression clues to determine the exact emotion. If a person is experiencing fear, the eyebrows will be raised and pulled together with tensed lower eyelids, while the two corners of their lips will appear stretched. Similarly, a person's surprise is expressed by eyebrows pulled up and a lowered jaw. Learn to read the entire face, especially micro expressions, if you want to learn more about how a person is feeling.

- Since micro expressions occur in fractions of seconds, they are virtually impossible to fake. For instance, notice how when people are being deceptive, their mouths will slightly angle differently. Similarly, their eye movements become more rapid, the nostrils flare a little bit, and they purse their lips together (a subconscious gesture signaling their lips are sealed, or they won't reveal the truth). Since these split expressions are driven by the subconscious, this makes them involuntary, and it is almost impossible to manipulate them.

- Enlarged pupils reveal intense emotions such as excitement, elation, delight, surprise, and interest. When a person is attracted to you or truly delighted to see you, their pupils will involuntarily enlarge.

- The direction of a person's feet can also determine what's going on in their mind. Since feet aren't the first thing on anyone's mind, it's harder to manipulate body language related to legs and feet. If a person's feet are pointing away from you, they are subconsciously signaling their need to escape. However, if their feet are pointed towards you, they are interested or in agreement with what you are saying.

- Typical signs of frustration and stress are clenched jaws, wrinkled eyebrows, and tensed neck. The person's words notwithstanding, if you observe any of these signs, he or she may be undergoing a stressful situation that they are trying to conceal. The trick for reading people's emotions accurately is to keep an eye out for a clear mismatch between verbal and non-verbal clues.

- Observe a person's walk to tune in to their feelings. People with a heavier gait along with low gravity while moving their legs are most likely hurt, stressed, frustrated, or depressed. People who walk with a slower and more relaxed pace are reflecting upon something. Notice how confident, happy, and goal-oriented people walk swiftly in one direction.

- Observing a person's eye movements is a near accurate way of gauging how he or she is feeling since our eye movements are connected to precise brain functions. Our eye movements have an established pattern depending on the brain function or type of information we are trying to access. For example, when a person is caught in an internal conflict or dilemma (to speak the truth or lie), they are more likely to look in the direction of their left collarbone. Darting sideways from one side to another can be a red flag that indicates deception.

- Proxemics is a subtopic within body language that talks about how people reveal their feelings and emotions through the physical distance they maintain with other people during the process of face-to-face interaction or communication. It is a very useful non-verbal signal for understanding a person's thought process or state of mind.

Psychologists and body language experts believe that the amount of physical distance we maintain while interacting with a person helps establish the dynamics of our relationship with them or reveals our emotions about them.

A person who isn't standing very close to you may not be emotionally open or receptive to you. They may have a tendency to closely guard their emotions or give only a little of themselves to the interaction. Such people may be more emotionally guarded and closed. You may need to make extra effort to get them to drop their guard and feel less intimidated. It may be a defense mechanism against being emotionally hurt or vulnerable.

On the other hand, if a person is leaning in your direction, they may subconsciously convey being emotionally open, or they trust you with their feelings. They may also be more interested in what you are speaking about.

Tone

The tone, volume, pitch, and emphasis of a person's voice can help you decode the hints that can help you tell what they are feeling. For example, if you notice plenty of inconsistencies in the tone of their voice as they speak, they are probably very angry, hurt, excited, or nervous. Ever notice how your voice shakes when you speak in a rage or are nervous about something? It can also be a sign the person is lying.

Similarly, if a person is speaking louder or softer than their regular volume, something may be amiss. Again, a person's tone is a dead giveaway. Sometimes people say something that sounds like a compliment. However, upon examining their tone closely, you realize the sarcasm and the condescension with which it was uttered.

The tone in which an individual ends their sentence says a lot about what they are trying to convey even with similar verbal clues. For example, if a person completes their sentence on a raised note, they are doubtful of something or are asking a question. Similarly, if they finish the sentence with a flat tone, they are pronouncing a statement or judgment. Watch out for how people end their sentences to get a clue about their inner feelings.

Again, the words people emphasize can help you uncover their true feelings. For example, if a person says, "Have you borrowed the blazer?" while emphasizing 'borrowed,' it indicates their doubt over whether you have borrowed, stolen, or done something else to the blazer. However, if the emphasis is on 'you,' they aren't sure if it is you or someone else who has borrowed the blazer.

I also like to look at pauses between phrases to know about the person's attitude, emotions, and intentions. For example, if a person pauses after saying something, it could be because what they just said is extremely important to them, or they truly believe in it. Sometimes, a person pauses to seek validation or feedback from others. The speaker wants to gauge your reaction to what they said since it is important for them.

When people are in a more emotionally unstable or negative frame of mind (angry, hurt, or upset), their voice tends to be higher pitched or squeaky. They are most likely losing a grip on their emotions or aren't able to regulate their emotions effectively. Notice how, when people are very angry, their voice becomes more screechy and squeaky, as if they are about to cry.

The speed of a speech

A person's emotions clearly impact the speed of their speech. Notice how you start talking much faster than your normal rate of speech, or words per minute, when you are angry or upset. A rapid speech can convey lack of organization, uncertainty, or lack of clarity. The person is not very comfortable with speaking and is just trying to finish throwing his or her words. Again, a slower than usual pace translates into low self-confidence, inability to express emotions, inability to come to terms with one's emotions, lack of emotional reassurance, and other similar feelings.

Verbal clues

A person's choice of words can say a lot about what they are thinking and feeling. Words are symbolic of our thoughts and feelings which, when combined with non-verbal clues, give us a comprehensive understanding of their emotional state.

The human brain is a miracle, really. When we think, or process rational and logical thoughts, we tend to use nouns and verbs. Conversely, when we attempt to express our thoughts or feelings in a verbal or written format, there is a tendency to use more adverbs and adjectives.

Any basic sentence features a subject and a verb. For example, "I walked." When a person adds more words to it, they can indicate their feelings or personality. For example, "I walked fast," can indicate a sense of urgency, fear, or insecurity. There are clear reasons why people use specific words over others.

Similarly, there is a hidden meaning behind what people say. Through their choice of words, people reveal emotions left unsaid.

Let's say you booked a table to take your family out for dinner at one of the fanciest, fine dining restaurants that recently opened in your neighborhood. The server greets you courteously and directs you to your table. What follows is an amazing dining experience.

The waiter introduces each of the seven courses in an informative yet engaging style, while you dine and enjoy wine in an upscale ambiance. After you enjoy a hearty meal and call for the tab, the waiter inquires if you enjoyed the food. You reply with, "The entrées were good."

The waiter doesn't look very delighted, even if what you said is a compliment in your opinion. Those four words you uttered reveal your real opinion about the food. It implies that other than the entrées, everything else was pretty average or the only thing that stood out during the entire meal were the entrées.

Did you actually say everything else other than the entrées was average? No. Then why did the waiter look crestfallen at your statement? It is obvious, people convey a lot not only through what they say but also through what they leave unsaid. Gather the hidden meaning or subtext behind what people say to tune in to their inner feelings. Notice how sometimes people will say, "You look very lovely today." It can either mean you look plain every day (which is a more passive-aggressive kind of statement), or you are looking exceptionally good today compared to other days.

Another powerful clue about what people are thinking or feeling is noticing how they talk about other people. In a research published in the *Journal of Personality and Social Psychology,* headed by Peter Harms and Simine Vazire of the University of Nebraska and University of St. Louis respectively, it was discovered that merely asking participants to rate positive and negative traits of three other people revealed a lot about the participants' social competence, general well-being, other people's perception of them, and their mental health.

It was observed that an individual's inclination to view other people in a positive manner was a strong indication of their own positive emotions. There is a strong link between seeing others in a more positive light and being emotionally stable, happy, productive, and enthusiastic.

On the other hand, viewing others in a negative light bears a strong correlation with a general sense of dissatisfaction, low self-esteem, anti-social behavior, and narcissism. People who hold plenty of negative emotions tend to perceive other people in a poorer or more negative light. This can also be an indication of emotional issues, mental health conditions, or a personality disorder. Again, emotions aren't good or bad but are reflections of how you are feeling. If a person experiences more negative emotions for others around them, it can be a clue to how they really feel about themselves.

If a person says that they 'made up their mind' after plenty of deliberation, the phrase indicates a mindset that is high on logic and rational thinking. The individual may be more contemplative and practical by nature. He or she may consider all the available options before making a decision. These are not your likely contenders for a snap of the moment decisions.

Do you know what metalanguage is? It is the intended words behind the words you speak. You don't say something directly but reveal it through the words you use. For example, notice how when people want to get someone to agree with what they've said, they'll always place yes, done, or okay followed by a question mark at the end. For example, "I can't hand in the project today. I'll submit it tomorrow, okay?" It is like manipulating the other person to agree.

To further increase your social-emotional quotient, pay attention to the sounds people utter, other than coherent words. Moaning, grunting, sighing, etc. can reveal a lot. Sometimes, these sounds will complement the words the speaker is using to make the message even more persuasive. However, at other times, there may be a mismatch between the person's words and sounds.

For example, someone may say, "I am having a really good day," followed by a sigh, which can indicate they are simply being sarcastic and are in fact having a bad day. You can even understand more about what a person really means when you observe their words and other miscellaneous sounds they make.

Environmental clues

A person's immediate environment says a lot about their emotional state. For instance, a messy, unclean, or disorganized space can indicate a lack of clarity of emotions or thoughts. Of course, everything has to be analyzed within a context. Someone may have an unkempt house because he or she is too busy to tidy it up and doesn't have housekeeping help.

All of us have certain spaces around us that are inaccessible that we don't really bother cleaning or organizing (space behind the cupboard or under the bed). These are spaces that we wouldn't normally clean. If such spaces are immaculately clean or organized, it can indicate anxiety or a disorder (obsessive-compulsive disorder).

Well-organized and clean spaces can indicate clarity of emotions or control over one's emotions. The person tends to be more reflective and introverted by nature. Similarly, people who are outwardly focused, or extroverts, tend to be surrounded by chaos.

This isn't pop psychology, but it is based on clear principles of how the environment around us is created through our actions, which themselves are directed by our subconscious thoughts and emotions. For example, using bright, vibrant, and bold prints in your décor or attire can be a sign of confidence, emotional self-assurance, and independence of thought or opinion. Likewise, a home with brighter and more vibrant colors is an indication of being bold, emotionally expressive, and outgoing. These people are not afraid of taking risks and are more than capable of understanding the needs and feelings of other people. More subtle colors imply inward directed emotions, or an introverted personality. These people may not be too receptive to another person's feelings and emotions.

People who hold on to old objects or hoard various objects can be excessively emotional, sensitive, or sentimental. They find it tough to move away from their past emotions or are still ridden by feelings of shame, regret, and guilt related to the past. These are people who latch on to old memories and can't release the emotions that hold them back.

When you use these verbal and non-verbal principles to understand people, your social-emotional quotient invariably increases.

Chapter Five: Secrets for Developing High Social E.I.

While our society is predictably emphasizing intelligence that is more tangible and visible (good grades), the one that goes largely overlooked and ignored is our ability to conduct ourselves in social situations. The knack of regulating our emotions in social settings in addition to being able to understand other people's feelings is our master key to success. While everyone is working hard on their book smarts, social smarts are also vital and, in fact, are proven to be more important than intelligence quotient.

Take for instance, a scenario where you are interviewing two candidates for a leadership role. Joanne is slightly more qualified, skilled, and experienced than Rose. However, Rose has the ability to understand people, works as a team player, and she can also inspire and motivate a team to accomplish higher targets. Joanne is high on technical skills but not very effective in understanding and managing people's emotions.

Who will you hire as a recruitment manager?

Obviously, Rose. The ability to understand and channel people's emotions in the best way possible is a priceless tool in today's world.

Social Intelligence (SI) is our ability to build relationships and figure out our way through social environments.

Here are some lesser known secrets that can increase your social-emotional intelligence by several fold:

Adopt and adapt

Don't fight your instinct to mirror another person's condition all the time. Human beings are wired to mirror the feelings and emotions of those around us. This is empathy! We naturally feel what others are feeling. However, at times we often the take the high road and try to fight this feeling of mirroring the other person's emotions. For example, say your spouse is upset and screaming at you. You know they are angry.

However, you've read how important it is to pacify the situation by not reacting in a similar manner. You choose to stay calm.

Then, you try to calm down your partner. This is where more trouble begins. The angry partner feels 'you don't understand them,' 'you don't understand what they are trying to say,' or 'you never get them.' In your view, you were simply trying to pacify the potentially volatile situation. How did it backfire?

This happens when, sometimes, instead of adapting to the emotions of the other person, we try to take the high road to fight mirroring their feelings. Rather, put yourself where your partner is and adopt his or her emotional state of mind. This may help you gain a good perspective of how they are feeling. It also helps them know that you understand where they are coming from, which makes the situation less unfriendly.

Practice being assertive, not aggressive

One of the secrets of being socially intelligent is learning to be more assertive without being aggressive. Assertive people know how not to please people all the time without offending them.

Assertiveness is a reasonable and genuine statement of opinions and feelings. "I would really prefer going to the games this weekend." This is an assertive statement.

You are making your needs clear without being aggressive or demanding. Aggressiveness is marked by a clear lack of respect for the needs and rights of other people. When you are aggressive, you are looking at things only from a selfish perspective or seeking to satisfy a self-filling goal. The aggressive version of the above statement would be, "We're good for the games this weekend."

You are pronouncing your statement more as a judgment without respect or concern for the other person.

On the other hand, assertiveness is characterized by respect and understanding for the other person's feelings or opinion, even though you may not agree with it. While aggressive says, "Only I am right," assertive says, "Though your opinion doesn't agree with mine, I respect it. We can agree to disagree."

Assertive people don't let others take advantage of them and know where to draw the line without being harsh. They know when to say 'no' to people without hurting their feelings. When you demonstrate respect for a person or group of people, the hurt is reduced. Assertive is making your stand clear while showing respect.

However, when you display lack of respect or concern for the other person's feelings, opinion, or desires, you are treading on aggression. Assertive people are unafraid of standing up for their values. They don't shy away from expressing their needs and goals to others. Assertive folks treat others as equals and operate from the point of mutual respect. They don't intend to hurt people and themselves. These are the people who are always seeking a win-win situation.

Aggressive people have a deep desire to win and operate from a point of disrespecting or overlooking other people's needs. They see hurting or disrespecting others as a by-product of winning or being successful. Aggressive folks are more focused on proving themselves right rather than arriving at a win-win solution. They have mastered the art of feeding on other people's insecurities and fears.

Social and emotional intelligence is about being assertive and respecting other people's needs and opinion while spelling out your own needs and opinion. As a leader, one must be assertive to make themselves clear while still showing respect and empathy towards the team. Even if you don't agree with someone, you must attempt to understand where they are coming from to boost your social-emotional quotient along with your social skills.

Here are some tips for boosting your assertiveness:

- **Keep communication genuine and open**

  Actively listen to the other person's opinions, needs, feelings, and desires. Watch out for verbal and non-verbal signals to understand them more effectively. Don't listen to respond or react, listen to understand. Similarly, listen without interrupting the other person. Let them finish what they say before you dive in with your take!

- **Don't be guilty**

  Don't feel guilty about refusing someone if it doesn't fit with your scheme of things. At the same time, listen to people without making them feel guilty for communicating their needs.

- **Stay calm and balanced**

  Even in a tense or potentially volatile situation, maintain eye contact, keep a relaxed expression, and speak in a steady, even tone. Assertive people seldom let their emotions control their actions. They have a good grip on themselves and can maintain composure even in the most stressful situations.

- **Practice assertiveness before a mirror**

  Pretend you are talking to a friend who is urging you to do something you don't want to do. How will you convey it to them in an open and honest manner? Focus on your words, body language, expressions, voice, and tone.

- **Always see people as allies and not enemies**

  In the workplace setting, think collaboration and not competition.

- **Stick with 'I' statements**

  For instance, instead of saying, "We should not go there," try saying, "I don't think we should go there." It makes you come across as firm without being pushy. You are expressing your thoughts without issuing a summons, which reveals respect for the other person.

- **Stay patient**

  If you are not an assertive person, it won't come overnight. Commit to being more mindful of your verbal and non-verbal communication while speaking to people for demonstrating greater assertiveness.

- **Respect differences in opinion**

  Realize that just because someone doesn't hold the same opinion as you, that doesn't mean he or she is wrong or bad. Agree to disagree and empathize with people even if you don't agree with them. Try to understand where they are coming from and what drives them to think the way they do.

Try to keep a win-win, problem-solution approach rather than proving your point or being obsessed with winning. During situations where you're in conflict with another person, avoid viewing the other person as an enemy. Rather, focus on a win-win solution that resolves the situation for everyone involved.

Practice empathy

Empathy is the ability to put yourself in someone else's shoes and feel their feelings or emotions exactly as they experience it. It is the ability to understand and experience other people's emotions as if it were happening to you. Predictably, the ability to experience other people's emotions and to leverage this experience for helping someone feel better about the situation is a much sought-after skill in today's world.

Empathy is the cornerstone of social-emotional intelligence. By empathizing with people, you can reach out to them and manage their emotions more efficiently. The ability to know how someone is feeling can be used to motivate, inspire, lead, and influence people in a positive manner.

Here are the top secrets for developing greater empathy:

- Traveling periodically to experience different places, cultures, lifestyles, and beliefs is a great way to develop empathy and appreciation for people whose lives are different from yours. You'll develop a better understanding and appreciation of people who are different from you. There will be a keener understanding of why they think and act the way they do.

- Examine your covert and overt biases. Most of us operate with certain biases centered on race, gender, age, education, profession, etc. They act as an obstacle when it comes to empathizing or listening to people. Make a list of biases that you think you possess and try to read opinions that are contrary to your biases. Look for evidence that challenges your thinking and gradually try to overcome these biases.

- Nurture a productive curiosity. You can learn something from an 'inexperienced subordinate,' a 'picky client,' or a 'hotheaded boss.' Rather than labeling people, develop a sense of curiosity about what you can genuinely learn from them. This will lead to a stronger understanding and appreciation of the people around you.

- Volunteer at an NGO or charity organization in your free time. It will not only help you appreciate what you already have but will also facilitate greater empathy for people who aren't as fortunate as you. The knowledge that you made a positive impact on someone's life will make you feel better about yourself. When you spend time with the less fortunate, you develop the ability to understand other people's challenges and problems, which in turn boosts your empathy factor.

- During situations where there is a conflict because of a difference in opinion, a resolution becomes easier when you understand the other party's underlying fears, needs, and motivations. Even when they are negative towards you, you'll understand why. Watch debates (especially during elections) to appreciate different points of view and understand why people think the way they do. If you find yourself tilting in any one direction, quickly look for evidence that is contrary to your stand. This will help you develop the ability to appreciate multiple points of view without being dogmatic about your stand. At its essence, empathy is about developing a greater understanding of another person's point of view or situation even when you don't necessarily agree with them.

- Practice predicting how a person will act or react in a certain situation by placing yourself in their shoes. This will give you greater insight and perceptiveness into how people feel about any given situation.

- Be fully present by keeping away your phone, turning off your email alerts, and mindfully listening to the other person. According to the research conducted by a professor at UCLA, things we speak make up for only seven percent of the message we are trying to communicate. The other 93 percent is determined by our body language and tone of voice. You are missing important clues if you aren't fully focusing on the other person while communicating with them.

They may be saying something that is contrary to what they feel, which you will miss if you are too preoccupied to focus on their non-verbal signals.

- Smiles are infectious. It rarely happens that someone smiles at you, and you don't smile in return. It the fastest way to connect with people and show solidarity or empathy towards them. A simple smile can boost feel-good hormones within the brain and stimulate its reward centers. You'll do yourself and others a whole lot of good by smiling.

- Address people by their names and praise them publicly. What is it that you heard about praising people publicly and admonishing them in private? Efficient leaders have mastered the art of using people's names while addressing them and using more encouraging statements. Make each person feel important by highlighting their skills or accomplishments in public. This inspires them to do even better work. Even when a person's performance slips, keep referring to accomplishments in public to remind them of their true potential. People respond wonderfully to praise.

- Give specific compliments to people. Your empathy and social-emotional quotient will increase when you learn to be more specific while appreciating people. For example, instead of saying, "You did a good job," tell someone, "The project was very well-researched and thorough despite the fact that the topic was complex and extensive," or, "Would you like to share the inspiration behind your brilliant sales growth concept?"

Be a listening champ

We saw how listening is intrinsic to the process of assertiveness and empathy, both of which are vital for boosting your social-emotional quotient.

Listening isn't only about hearing out what people are saying. It is also figuring out what they leave unspoken through their body language, voice, emotions, and choice of words. Let us consider an example to better understand how listening (or tuning in to verbal and non-verbal patterns) is integral to the process of communication.

It's Friday evening, and after a hectic week at work, everyone is getting ready to let their hair down over the weekend. They are shutting down their computers and getting ready to leave when the company CEO, Sue, walks in and informs them that the deadline for the project they've been working so hard on is pushed ahead by two weeks.

Everyone is naturally disappointed and stressed. The project head sits silently at her desk wondering how to comply with the deadline. The project manager, Ann, says, "We will still do a good job and submit the project according to the new deadline." Another employee, Dan, gets to work on his computer, and few people leave the office. A majority of team members say they can handle the new adjustments. Sue leaves the office thinking like it went way better than she thought it would.

What she didn't catch was the inconsistency in the body language and words of the project manager, who left the office in a rage, while she replied to an email from a prospective recruiter. Other team members went to grab a coffee and were almost in tears from the newfound stress they will face.

Yes, no one told Sue how they truly felt when she asked for feedback. So, how was she supposed to know how they really felt about the deadline being pushed? Do you think she was in any way responsible for not understanding her employees' feelings? Of course, she didn't really listen or tune in to what they were trying to convey. She went by their words but failed to catch what they left unsaid. A major part of social-emotional intelligence is to understand what people leave unsaid.

Here are some tips to develop ace listening skills:

- Keep an open mind. Avoid operating with a pre-conditioned, or prejudiced, mind and be more open to listening to people without labeling or criticizing them. I'd say one of the biggest challenges in the process of communication is listening to people without jumping to conclusions. Don't attempt to hijack the conversation or try to finish their sentences. Remember, the person is communicating their ideas, thoughts, opinions, and feelings. Let them freely express themselves without being interrupted.

- We often spend more time planning what we are going to say in response to something rather than actively listening to a person to understand them. Don't listen to respond. Listen to understand what the person is trying to convey. Focus completely on what the speaker is saying rather than rehearsing your responses. Even if something seems uninteresting, listen to it.

- Wait for the speaker to pause before asking questions or clarifying doubts. Don't interrupt someone in the middle of their speech. Rather, hold your questions until they pause. "Let us go back a few seconds. I didn't really understand what you meant by XYZ." Sometimes our questions can throw people in a totally different direction from where they intend to take the conversation. When the speaker is going in a different direction, get them back on the original topic by saying something like, "It was wonderful knowing about ABC, but tell us more about XYZ now."

Conclusion

Thank you for making it through to the end of this book, let's hope it was informative and was able to provide you with all the tools you need to achieve your goals.

I hope you enjoyed reading it and that you were able to learn the finer aspects of emotional intelligence, self-awareness, and social relationships. I also hope it offered you plenty of inspiring ideas, practical tips, and nuggets of wisdom about boosting your emotional quotient, or emotional intelligence.

The best part is, unlike intelligence quotient, emotional quotient can be developed through regular practice, training, and application. Improving your emotional intelligence is a continuous and dynamic process that helps you enhance your skills over time.

The next step is to simply go out there and use all the proven strategies mentioned in the book. You can't become more emotionally intelligent overnight by reading about it. Apply the techniques mentioned in the book in your everyday life to witness results!

You'll gradually transform from an emotionally incompetent individual who struggles with their own and other people's emotions to an emotionally evolved and socially adept individual, who will enjoy better interpersonal relationships and professional success in life.

Finally, if you found this book useful in any way, a review on Amazon is always appreciated!

95314763R00057

Made in the USA
Middletown, DE
25 October 2018